A Handbook of Oral French

A Complete Guide to Spoken French

By
Phil Beth

Author of Do-It-Yourself French

Phil Beth

Copyright © October 2022. Phil Beth

All Rights Reserved.

This work took loads of punishing research and resources. Transmission of this work in any way is not really the best idea. If you feel an acquaintance needs to have it, please consider recommending its purchase to them.

For criticism and suggestions, please send an email to francaissimplifie.biz@gmail.com.

If you think someone needs to have this book, don't just recommend it for free. Send an email to francaissimplifie.biz@gmail.com to get an affiliate link.

Phil Beth

Table of Contents

Preface

Section I
Certain First Principles

Section II
The Vowels

Section III
The Consonants

Section IV
The Role of the Accents

Section V
Silent Letters

Section VI
Pronunciation Across Word Boundaries and the Associated Processes

Section VII
Stress and Intonation

Section VIII
Exceptions to Common Rules

Phil Beth

Detailed Table of Contents

Chapters	Topics	Pages
Preface	The Sound System of French	7
	Transcription Key	8
SECTION I: CERTAIN FIRST PRINCIPLES		
1	• The Alphabet • Difference between letters and sounds	10 11
2	An Overview of the IPA Symbols of French	13
3	• Units of French Pronunciation • The Rhythmic Group	16 19
SECTION II: THE VOWELS		
4	The Vowels	23
5	/e/ and /ɛ/	27
6	[i], [u] and [y]	37
7	[ə] or The Schwa	43
8	[a], [ɑ], [ɑ̃] and [ɛ̃]	46
9	[ø], [œ] and [œ̃]	51
10	[o], [ɔ] and [ɔ̃]	54
11	Semi-vowels	58
12	Vowel Length	62
SECTION III: THE CONSONANTS		

13	• Consonants • Voiced Consonants and Voiceless Consonants • Consonant Clusters	64 65 66
14	[b] and [p]	69
15	[d] and [t]	72
16	[ʃ] and [ʒ]	75
17	[f] and [v]	78
18	[g] and [k]	81
19	[l], [m] and [n]	84
20	[ɲ] and [ŋ]	88
21	[ʁ]	90
22	[s] and [z]	92
SECTION IV: THE ROLE OF THE ACCENTS		
23	The Accents: Why They Matter .	97
SECTION V: SILENT LETTERS		
24	Silent Letters	103
25	Aspiration of H	106
SECTION VI: PRONUNCIATION ACROSS WORD BOUNDARIES AND THE ASSOCIATED PROCESSES		
26	Liaison	109
27	Mandatory Liaison	113
28	Verb Conjugations and Liaison • Third Person Verb Inversion and Liaison • First-Person-	116 116

		Singular -Verb Inversion and Liaison	117
		• First-Person-Singular -Verb Inversion in -er verbs	118
		• The Imperative Mood and Liaison	118
29		Forbidden and Optional Liaisons	121
30		Elision	125
31		Enchaînement	128
32		Gemination	131
SECTION VII: INTONATION AND STRESS			
33		Intonation and Stress	134
SECTION VIII: EXCEPTIONS TO COMMON RULES			
34		Irregular Pronunciation Patterns	138
35		Informal Pronunciation	141
36		Cases of Special Pronunciation	144
Appendix		Full List of Aspirated H Words	146

Phil Beth

Preface

Sound System of French
The Sound System of French or French Phonology is the method employed in spoken French. It is not merely the vowels and consonants involved but also the processes and styles that shape the overall production of speech in French. The three processes are: Liaison, elision and enchaînement. Stress and Intonation are also an important element of well-produced speech in French.

It is clearly evident that written and spoken French appear to be two distinct languages, hence the need to master the art of speaking French fluently.
In view of this, this book has been prepared for English speakers trying to master oral French with special emphasis on those areas that are strange to us.
Fortunately, Oral French is no rocket science, no, not in the least, so get your speech organs ready and poised for what maybe unfamiliar and see yourself a winner. On y va !

Phil Beth

Phil Beth

Transcription Key for this Book

IPA sounds are enclosed within square brackets or slashes.

A colon (:) after a vowel shows that the vowel is long.

A dot (.) divides a phonetic transcription into syllables.

Section I
CERTAIN FIRST PRINCIPLES

Chapter 1
The Alphabet

French has the alphabet letters as English. This means there are 26 alphabet letters in French and they are:
A B C D E F G H I J K L M N O P Q R S T U V W X Y Z

However, the French pronunciation is different:

A………………../ah/
B………………../beh/
C………………../seh/
D………………../deh/
E………………../ə/
F………………../ef/
G………………../jay/
H………………../ash/
I………………../ee/
J………………../jee/
K………………../kah/
L………………../el/
M………………../em/
N………………../en/
O………………../o/
P………………../pay/
Q………………../kiu/

R………………../erh/
S………………../es/
T………………../tay/
U………………../iu/
V………………../vay/
W………………../doobluh-vay/
X………………../iks/
Y………………../iygrek/
Z………………../zayd/

Difference between Letters and Sounds

Succinctly put, letters are for spelling while sounds or phonemes are for speaking. In this book, Sounds are written between two slashes / / or within square brackets [ ].

Chapter 2
An Overview of the IPA Symbols of French

There are more than 100 sounds in the International Phonetic Alphabet (IPA). However, only 38 of them are used in French. The 38 sounds or phonemes are grouped into 3 categories namely:
1. Vowels
2. Semi-vowels
3. Consonants

Table 2.0: French IPA Phonemes.

IPA	Examples
Consonants	
[b]	B as in beau
[d]	D as in dans
[f]	F as in fer
[g]	G as in gâteau
[ʒ]	G as in manger
[k]	C as in cadeau
[l]	L as in village
[m]	M as in mère
[n]	N as in donner
[ŋ]	NG as in camping
[ɲ]	GN as in gagner

A Handbook of Oral French

[p]	P as in père
[ʁ]	Cher
[s]	S as in salutation
[ʃ]	CH as in chanter
[t]	T as in trop
[v]	V as in vin
[z]	Z as in zéro
Vowels	
[a]	A as in ta.
[ɑ]	Â as in âge.
[e]	É as in né
[ɛ]	-AI- as in mais,
[ɛː]	Aî as in maître
[ə]	E as in je.
[ø]	-EU as in eux,
[œ]	Œ as in sœur
[i]	I as in si
[ɔ]	O as in forte
[o]	AU as in chaud
[u]	OU as in beaucoup
[y]	U as in tu
[ɑ̃]	-AN- as in enfant,
[ɛ̃]	-IN- as in vin
[œ̃]	-UN- as in brun.
[ɔ̃]	-ON- as in ton,
Semi-vowels	
[w]	OU + vowel, as in Oui.

Phil Beth

| [j] | Y as in yeux |
| [ɥ] | UI as in nuit |

Chapter 3
Units of French Pronunciation

We shall discuss three levels of sound organization in French.

1. The Phoneme
These are the individual sounds of French. They are the individual vowels, semi-vowels and consonants listed in chapter 1. There are 38 phonemes in French.

2. The Syllable
A syllable is a unit of sound made up of a vowel, a vowel and one consonant or a vowel between two consonants. In phonetic transcription, a dot is used to separate syllables.

Par exemple :
1. Or /ɔː/ makes one syllable.
2. Be /biː/ makes one syllable
3. Bet /bet/ makes one syllable.
4. Boutique /bu.tiːq/ makes two syllables.

- ***Open , Closed and Full Syllables***

An open syllable ends with a vowel as in 1 and 2 in the examples above and also the first syllable in boutique.
On the other hand, a closed syllable ends with a consonant as in example 3 above and the second syllable in boutique.
A full syllable is a syllable that has a vowel that is not the schwa.

French Syllabification

French prefers open syllables to closed ones. So, a word is divided into as many open syllables as possible. Note that syllables and syllabification are a phonetic thing. This means that you break up words into syllables according to how they are pronounced and not how they are spelt. Sounds are considered, not letters.
Rule
If a consonant occurs between two vowel sounds, the consonant is in the same syllable as the second vowel.

Table 3.0: Division of Words into Syllables

Words	Syllables
Après	A|prés
Assez	As|sez
Oiseau	Oi|seau
Gâteau	Gâ|teau
Cadeaux	Ça|deaux
Beaucoup	Beau|coup

| Manger | Man\|ger |
| Haricots | Ha\|ri\|cots |

Monosyllables,, Disyllables and Polysyllables

A monosyllable is a monosyllabic word and has only one syllable.
Examples are:
À
Ce
De
Que
Je
Il
Elle
Vin
Le
La
Me
Te
Se
Qui
Nuit
Fou
Cette
Cet
Ces
Les
Où
Chat

A disyllable is disyllabic and has two syllables.
Examples:
Après
Assez
Oiseau
Gâteau
Cadeaux
Beaucoup
Manger
Souris
A polysyllable is polysyllabic and has three syllables or more.
Examples:
Attention
Haricots
États-Unis

3. The Rhythmic Group

In a French sentence, words are not pronounced one by one but rather in blocs or rhythmic groups. A rhythmic group is a phrase made up of syntactically related words that are pronounced at one go (as if they were one word) . A rhythmic group is made up of 3-7 syllables. If a sentence is short, two phonological phrases may be merged.

Basic Types of Rhythmic Groups
1. ***Noun Group***: This comprises a noun or a noun phrase.

Examples
- Pierre
- Un autre homme
- Un bel oiseau
- Marseille
- Luc et Jean
- Mes amis
- Ma mère
- La reine, etc

2. ***Verbal Group***: This is made up of verbs.

Examples
Va aller
Voulais me jeter
Veux aller manger

3. ***Subject Pronoun-Verb Group***: Single subject pronouns are included in a verbal group to make a subject pronoun-verb group.

Examples
- Ils sont partis.
- J'ai eu
- Tu as acheté

4. ***Prepositional Group:*** This includes a preposition and the noun it precedes.

Examples

Dans une maison

Aux États-Unis

En Angleterre.

Table 3.1: Parsing Sentences into Rhythmic Groups

Sentence	Division into Rhythmic Groups
Il sont partis à l'école .	Il sont partis | à l'école .
Pierre et Jean vont aller jouer au basket.	Pierre et Jean | vont aller jouer | au basket.
Mes parents vont manger dans leur chambre.	Mes parents | vont manger | dans leur chambre.
Nos amis français voudraient manger des haricots pour le déjeuner	Nos amis français | voudraient manger | des haricots | pour le déjeuner.

Characteristics of Rhythmic Groups

1. Liaisons occur mainly within rhythmic groups.

2. Enchaînement also happens within rhythmic groups.

Liaison and Enchaînement are elaborately discussed in later chapters.

SECTION II

VOWELS

Chapter 4
The Vowels

Vowels are those sounds that are produced without any obstruction in the airways due to contact between speech organs. In other words, vowel sounds are made without any two speech organs making contact.

Table 4.0: Vowels

Oral Vowels	
[a]	A as in ta.
[ɑ]	Â as in âge.
[e]	É as in né
[ɛ]	-AI-as in mais,
[ɛː]	Aî as in maître
[ə]	E as in je.
[ø]	-EU as in eux,
[œ]	Œ as in sœur
[i]	I as in si
[ɔ]	O as in forte
[o]	AU as in chaud
[u]	OU as in beaucoup
[y]	U as in tu
Nasal Vowels	
[ɑ̃]	-AN- as in enfant,
[ɛ̃]	-IN- as in vin
[œ̃]	-UN- as in brun.
[ɔ̃]	-ON- as in ton,

French vowels are divided into two:
1. Oral vowels.
2. Nasal vowels.

Oral Vowels

Oral vowels are produced with air moving through the mouth alone. There 12 of them as shown below .

Table 4.1: Oral Vowels

IPA	Examples
[a]	A as in ta
[ɑ]	Â as in âge.
[e]	É as in né
[ɛ]	-AI-as in mais.
[ɛː]	Aî as in maître
[ə]	E as in je.
[ø]	-EU as in eux.
[œ]	Œ as in sœur
[i]	I as in si
[ɔ]	O as in forte
[o]	AU as in chaud
[u]	OU as in beaucoup
[y]	U as in tu.

Nasal Vowels

Nasal Vowels are produced by making air leave through the mouth and the nose at the same time. . There are 4 of them as shown and they will be discussed in more detail in later chapters.

Table 4.2: Nasal Vowels

[ɑ̃]	-AN- as in enfant.
[ɛ̃]	-IN- as in vingt
[œ̃]	-UN- as in brun.
[ɔ̃]	-ON- as in ton.

Semi-vowels

Also called semi-consonants, semi-vowels are intermediate between vowels and consonants in that there is only a partial, weak obstruction to airflow in their articulation. There are 3 semi-vowels in French as shown in the table below.

Table 4.3: Semi-vowels

[w]	OU + vowel as in Ouest.
[j]	Y as in yeux
[ɥ]	UI between consonants as in nuit

Phil Beth

Chapter 5
/e/ and /ɛ/

[e]

This sound is the sound of the e in hey, just before you glide to y. It is a short vowel except when followed by v, z, r, vr or a soft g, in which case it becomes long.

Table 5.0: How [e] is Spelt in Words

Letters	Words
E at the beginning of words (provided there is no cluster of two consonants immediately after. However, if one of the two consonants is r, the E remains /e/)	Eveil
	Essuyer
	Effaré
	Effacer
	Effectuer
	Effectif
	Efféminé
	Effigie
	Effet
	Effervescent
	Efficace
	Effilé
	Effilocher
	Effondrer
	Efforcer
	Effort
	Effroi
	Effriter

	Effréné
	Effusion
	Essai
	Essence
	Essieu
	Essaim
	Essor
	Essorer
	Essouffler
é	Mangé
	Acheté
	Élevé
	Dansé
	Étape
	Ébréché
	Éclat
	Changé
	Dégager
	Défi
	Détail
	Antérieur
	Fée
	Édimbourg
	Fusée
	Caché
	Passé
	Rêvé
	Allé
	Musclé
	Crée
	Lié

	Marché
	Église
	École
	Partagé
	Étrange
	Asséché
-ER at the end of verbs	Danser
	Manger
	Marcher
	Acheter
	Préparer
	Écouter
	Aller
	Essayer
	Chanter
	Sauter
	Cuisinier
	Frapper
	Gifler
	Garder
	Apporter
	Porter
	Cacher
	Trouver
	Aider
	Détester
	Appliquer
	Expliquer
	Gifler
	Préférer
	Aimer

	Tutoyer
	Porter
	Emmener
	Amener
	Protéger
	Jeter
	Appeler
	Pleurer
	Flanquer
	Planquer
	Souhaiter
	Exercer
-ez	Assez
	Mangez
	Allez
	Achetez
	Dépêchez
	Donnez
	Trouvez
	Chez
	Venez
	Écrivez
	Avez
	Croyez
	Souhaitez
	Apprenez
	Comprenez
	Voulez
	Pouvez
	Entrez
	Mentez

	Savez Sauvez Connaissez Haïssez
-es	Les Ces Des Mes Tes
Ê (provided it is not in the last syllable.)	Mêler Évêché Dépêtrer Dépêcher Gêner Têtu
Ay	Ayons Ayez Pays Essayer Effrayé Égayer
-ef	Clef
-ed	Pied
Ë	Canoë
ei	Beignet
et	Et

	Beignet
	Muet
Ai (provided the next syllable contains /e/ or /y/ also)	Aimer.
	Dégainer
	Entraîner
	Aigu
	Aiguilles

[ɛ]

This vowel has the same sound as the e in fed. It is a short vowel. It becomes long when followed by r, v, z ,vr or a soft l a closed, stressed syllable.

Table 5.1: How [ɛ] is Spelt in Words

Letters	Words
È	Père
	Mère
	Achète
	Frère
	Genève
	Obèse
	Grève
	Élève
	Genèse

	Aiguière
	Allègre
	Espèce
	Allergène
	Allège
	Antithèse
	Bijoutière
	Ère
	dernière, amèrement
	parlèrent
	Étagère
	Étrangère
	Galère
	Oeillères
	Gène
	Gangrène
	Fière
	Fièvre
	Arrière
When e flanks double consonants	Fesse
	Jette
	Elle
	Benne
	Sagesse
	Appelle
	Prenne
	Vienne
	Cette
	Cassette
	Muette
ei	Neige

	Beige
	Beigne
	Eveil
	Reine
	Peigne
	Peine
	Baleine
	Seigneur
	Seiche
	Seize
	Seine
	Seigle
Ê in the last syllable	Être
	Évêque
	Genêt
	Prêt
	Même
	Quête
	Forêt
	Bête
	Benêt
	Gêne
	Ancêtre
	Arrête
	Dépêche
	Enquête
Ë at any position	Noël
Ai (provided the vowel in the next	Aimant J'ai

syllable is not /e/)	Sais Lait Dégaine Entraînant
-et	Effet Octet Jouet Gilet Alphabet Billet Muguet Sujet
E (provided there is a cluster of two consonants following immediately. The two consonants must not include r .), Followed by a pronounced l in the last syllable.	Eczéma Esprit Estimer Gestion Estival Est Gestation Excès Exclure Sélect Exercer Espoir Esquiver Esclave Escroc Espace Espérer Espagne

	Escale
	Exemple
	Exposer
	Exprès
	Exercice
	Extraire
	Sel
-er + consonant	Ouvert
	Offert

[ɛː]

This is the long version of [ɛ]. It is found in words like fête and maître.

Chapter 6
[i], [u] and [y]

The Vowel [i]

This simple vowel sounds like the I in "it" but is a bit longer. It becomes a long vowel when it is immediately (and separately) followed by a soft g, v, z, r or vr in a stressed, closed syllable. Note that if [i] is followed by a cluster of the listed sounds, it remains a short vowel. Also, when it is followed by all other consonants, it remains short.

Table 6.0: How [i] is Spelt in Words

Letters	Words
I (including all accented variants and when followed by an unaccented e) at the initial position, between consonants, after u or preceded by a consonant or u at the final position. In every case, it must not be followed by n or m.	Île Fini Endurcit Fille Fils Lire Dire Idée Illogique Ils Illuminé Sorti If Igné

	Igname
	Image
	Illusion
	Imiter
	Cieux
	Lumière
	Exil
	Huit
	Nuit
	Partie
	Système
	Syphilis lusione
	Idioties
	Habiter
	Zizi
	Zombi
	Vomir
	Volubilis
Ï at any position except in -ïn+ consonant and ïm+ consonant	Maïs
	Jamaïque
	Haïti
	Faïence
	Haïr
	Judaïsme
	Héroïque
	Ambiguïté
	Inouï
	Cocaïne
Hi	Envahir
	Hibou
	Trahir

	Hiver
	Histoire
Y before or between consonants and after a In both cases, it must not be followed by n or m or a vowel.	Dynamique
	Dynamite
	Y croire
	Pays
	Pyramide
	Hymne
	Stylo
	Dynamo
	Dysenterie
	Dynastie
	Dyslexique

[u]

This is the familiar sound of the -ou- in boutique. It is a short vowel except when followed by r, v, z, vr or a soft g in a closed, stressed syllable.

Table 6.1: How [u] is Spelt in Words

Letters	Words
OU, including OÙ between consonants or at the end of a word	Beaucoup
	Tout
	Pour
	Pouvez
Also -oue at the end of a word.	Fou
	Jour
	Toujours

	Lourd
	Loup
	Coup
	Ou
	Où
	Coucou
	Coucher
	Douche
	Trouver
	Sous
	Mourir
	Nourriture
	Retour
	Bijoux
	Bisous
	Amour
	Nous
	Vous
	Nouveau
	Avoue

[y]

There is no similar sound to this in English. It is described as a rounded /i/. To articulate this sound, try articulating [i] as if it were [u]. You get a sound at the back of your throat that is midway between /i/ and /u/. Another way to go about this sound is this: Make as if to say /iu/ but stop halfway through your glide to /u/.

Table 6.2: How [y] is Spelt in Words

Letters	Words
U between consonants and at the final position, Also heard in -une but never in -un. -ue at the end of a word	Tu Du Sur Dessus Su Vu Reçu États-Unis Une Lune. Jupe Mue Cocu Juste Jute Juguler
Eu in past forms of avoir	Il eut Ils eurent J'ai eu Elle l'a eue.

Chapter 7
[ə] or The Schwa

This sound, also called the schwa, is the short, weak sound of the a in "above". In French, it is also referred to as e muet (mute e). This sound is found in an e with no accent on it. The following are instances where the schwa is realized:
1. At the end of one-syllable words like je, ce, de, le etc.
2. When e is followed by a single consonant within a word e.g. appeler, fenêtre, etc.

The e at the end of words with more than one syllable like monde is usually dropped except in versification.

Table 7.0: How [ə] is Spelt in Words

Letters	Words
Unaccented e in monosyllables or between consonants in polysyllables. This does not include -er.	Acheté
Je
Le
De
Ce
Me
Te
Se
Petite

	Jeter
	Regarder
	Demain
	Dessus
	Dessous
	Fenêtre
	Benêt
	Mener
	Selon
	Grelot
-ai in disyllabic conjugations of faire.	Faisant Faisons
On	Monsieur
Eu	Euro (currency)

Some Words in Which the Unaccented e is Silent
Sorcellerie
 Amener,
Emmener
Dysenterie,
Élever,
Jugement
Bienvenue
Sûreté
Parement

Chapter 8
[a], [ɑ], [ɑ̃] and [ɛ̃]

[a]
This is the sound of the a in trap. It is a short vowel except when followed by v,z, r vr or a soft g.

[ɑ]
This sound is [a] made further back in the mouth. Hence, [ɑ] is commonly called 'back a'. It is the sound of the a when people in the UK say "ask" . It is a short vowel except when followed by a consonant in a closed stressed syllable in which case it becomes long.

[ɑ̃]
To make this sound, simply produce [ɑ] while letting air pass through the nose at the same time. This nasal is a short vowel except when followed by a consonant in a closed stressed syllable.

[ɛ̃]
To make this sound, simply exclaim "ah!" while letting air pass through the nose at the same time.

Phil Beth

It is a short vowel except when followed by a consonant in a closed, stressed syllable.

Table 8.0: How [a] is Spelt in Words

Letters	Words
A, including all accented variants except â.	À Arbre Havre Gagner Armes Patrimoine Fax Examen Paris Parement
A before -tion in bisyllabic words	Nation
-em- in -emme-	Femme Apparemment Évidemment Différemment Ardemment

Table 8.1: How [a] is Spelt in Words

Letters	Words
A	The alphabet letter A
Â	Pâte Bâiller Bâillon Bâton

	Hâte
	Tâte
	Gâter
	Gâteau
	Tâtonné
	Tâche
	Gâcher
	Âme
A before final -tion in polysyllabic words.	Condamnation Éducation Déclaration Gestation Formation

Table 8.2: How [ã] is Spelt in Words.

Letters	Words
-an- between consonants, between an accented e and a consonant, followed by a consonant at the beginning of a word, in the last syllable of a word	Enfant Bienséance
-en- between consonants, Followed by a consonant at the	Enfant Mentir Gens Lendemain

A Handbook of Oral French

beginning of a word, In the last syllable of a word.	
-am- before or between consonants	Shampooing Champ Chambre

Table 8.3: How [ɛ̃] is Spelt in Words

Letters	Words
-in- • Followed by a consonant at the beginning or end of a word. • Between consonants ,	Vingt Vin Brin Fin Divin Shampooing Intelligent
-im- followed by a consonant	Important Simple Joachim
-ein- + consonant or at the end of a word	Plein
-aim- + consonant or at the end of a word	Faim
-ain- + consonant Or in the last syllable	Pain Sainte Bain
-yn or ym + consonant	Sympa Syntaxe Syndicat

	Syncope
	Symptôme
	Synthèse
	Thym
-en- preceded by i in the last syllable of a word	Viens
	Bien
-en-	Benjamin
	Moyen
	Agenda
	Examen
	Mémento

Chapter 9
[ø], [œ] and [œ̃]

[ø]

This is another unfamiliar sound. To produce this vowel, the sound e is articulated with the mouth rounded. It is a short vowel except when followed by a consonant in a stressed, closed syllable.

Table 9.0: How [ø] is Spelt in Words

Letters	Words
-eu in the last open syllable	Peu Peut Queue
Eux	Odieux Heureux Joyeux
Eur + vowel	Europe Eurocrate

[œ]

This is similar to the sound of the -ur- in church. In closed, stressed syllables, it becomes long when followed by r, v, z, vr or a soft g.

Table 9.1: How [œ] is Spelt in Words

Letters	Words
eur	Beurre Heur Humeur Secteur Peur Organisateur
œu	Cœur Sœur
-eu- between consonants	Peuvent Peuple Fleuve Neuf

[œ̃]

To make this sound, simply produce [œ] while letting air pass through the nose at the same time. It is a short vowel except when followed by a consonant in a closed, stressed syllable.

Table 9.2: How [œ̃] is Spelt in Words

Letters	Words
-un- between consonants and at the end of a word	Un Lundi Chacun

Chapter 10
[o], [ɔ] and [õ]

[o]

This is the sound of the o in the American English "go" just before the glide to /u/. It is a short vowel except when followed by a consonant in a closed, stressed syllable. It is described as articulated by keeping the lips perfectly round.

Table 10.0: How [o] is Spelt in Words

Letters	Words
Ô	Hôtel
	Hôpital
	Tôt
	Côte
	Aube
	Geôlier
O in the last open syllable	Sot
	Flot
	Photo
	Fluo
	Coco
AU between consonants or in the last syllable of a word	Chaussures
	Chaud
	Faux
	Aujourd'hui
	Faute

	Ébauche
	Déchausser
	Soubresaut
EAU	Eau
	Beaucoup
	Beau
	Seaux
	Jumeau

[ɔ]

This sound is the sound of the o in pot. It is a short vowel. It only becomes long if followed by v, r, z, vr or a soft g in a closed, stressed syllable.

Table 10.1: How [ɔ] is Spelt in Words

Letters	Words
O + double consonants + e	Pomme
	Homme
	Cocotte
	Hotte
	Flotte
	Abandonné
O + consonant except m or n.	Cote
	Porter
	Photo
	Sort
	Mort

	Génocide
	Coche
	Cocotte
	Obtenir
	Coco
	Haricots
	Note
u (*rare*)	Summum

[õ]

To make this sound, simply produce [ɔ] while letting air pass through the nose as well as through the mouth. It is a short vowel except when followed by a consonant in a closed stressed syllable.

Table 10.2: How [õ] *is Spelt in Words*

Letters	Words
-on- between consonants, before a consonant, and in the last syllable of a word	Oncle Son Mon On Bon
-om- between consonants (provided it is not followed by n	Somptueux Somptuaire Sombre

| +vowel) | |

Chapter 11
Semi-vowels

[j]

This sound is the sound of the y in "you". Apart from the letter y, it is found in glides from /i/ to another vowel.

Table 11.0: How [j] is Spelt in WWord

Letters	Words
Y at the beginning of words	Yeux
Y between vowels	Soyez
-ille in the last syllable.	Fille Juillet Oeillet Ville Ouille Travailler Surveiller
-il at the end of a word (provided the preceding letter is a vowel)	Oeil Travail Bercail
-ill- + vowel other	Oeillade

than e (provided -ill- is preceded by a vowel)	Oeillères Bienveillance Jaillir
-I + full vowel (i.e a vowel sound other than the schwa) Provided it is preceded by a consonant	Hier Cahier Nié Courtier Sommier Dernier Sérieux

[w]

This is the same familiar sound of the w in "water". Apart from the letter w, it is found in glides from /u/ to another vowel.

Table 11.1: How [w] is Spelt in Words

Letters	Words
W	Week-end
Ou + vowel or h	Oui Ouais Souhait Louer Éboueur
O + i or y, in which case it forms the diphthong /wa/ . If it is -oin + consonant or in an open syllable, the	Soi Soin Loi Loin Toi

diphthong is /wɛ̃/	Soyez
	Moyen
	Moi
	Mois
	Moins
	Coins

|ɥ|

This sound, shown as an inverted h turned the other way left, is quite unfamiliar to English speakers. It is a glide from /y/ to another vowel. It is commonly as a merger of [j] and [w]. To produce it, say [j] while keeping your lips a bit rounded.

Or you could start with [j] and glide halfway through to [w].

Letters	Words
-u- + vowel	Nuit
	Huit
	Suis
	Tua
	Tuer
	Arguer

Chapter 12
Vowel Length

By default, all French vowels are short except [ɛː]. Vowels lengthen their duration if they are in the final closed, full syllable of the last word in a rhythmic group. They do so under these conditions:
1. [o], [ø], [ɑ], [ɑ̃], [ɔ̃], [ɛ̃], and [œ̃] are lengthened before any consonant.
   Examples
   pâte [pɑːt],
   chante [ʃɑ̃ːt] .
2. All vowels are lengthened if followed by /v/, /z/, /ʒ/, /ʁ/ (not in combination) or by /vʁ/.
   Examples
   mère [mɛːʁ]
   crise [kʁiːz]
   livre [liːvʁ]

However, words such as (ils) servent [sɛʁv] or tarte [taʁt] are pronounced with short vowels since the /ʁ/ appears in clusters other than /vʁ/.

Phil Beth

SECTION III

THE CONSONANTS

Chapter 13
Consonants

The Consonants are those sounds that are heard when two or more speech organs make contact. Most French consonants are already familiar to us because they are also used in English. There are 18 consonants in French as shown in the table below.

Table 13.0: French Consonant Phonemes

[b]	B as in beau
[d]	D as in dans
[f]	F as in fer
[g]	G as in gâteau
[ʒ]	G as in manger
[k]	C as in cadeau
[l]	L as in village
[m]	M as in mère
[n]	N as in donner
[ŋ]	NG as in camping
[ɲ]	GN as in gagner
[p]	P as in père
[ʁ]	Cher
[s]	S as in salutation
[ʃ]	CH as in chanter
[t]	T as in trop

[v]	V as in vin
[z]	Z as in zéro

Voiced consonants and Voiceless consonants.

12 of the French consonants are paired up as voiced and voiceless. Each voiced consonant has a voiceless double.
What is a Voiced Consonant?
If a consonant triggers vibration in the vocal cords (the throat), it is described as voiced. If it does not, it is voiceless. To check for voiced/voiceless status of a consonant, place a finger on the throat. If a movement is felt, then it is voiced; if no movement is felt, it is voiceless. In the table below, each voiced consonant is paired with its voiceless version.

Table 13.1: Voiced and Voiceless Consonants Pairs

Voiced	Voiceless
[b]	[p]
[ʒ]	[ʃ]
[d]	[t]
[g]	[k]

[v]	[f]
[z]	[s]
[m]	No pair
[n]	No pair
[l]	No pair
[ʁ]	No pair
[ŋ]	No pair
[ɲ]	No pair

Consonant Clusters

When two or more consonants appear together in the pronunciation of a word without an intervening vowel, they are said to be *clustered*. Note that x within a word usually represents a /ks/ cluster or a /gz/ cluster

Examples of Words with consonant clusters include

Grand

Esprit

E**x**ercice

General Features
   1. **Non-Aspiration**

The familiar consonants of French are articulated like in English. The only difference is that the French ones are not aspirated. This means there is no burst of breath in their articulation as we do in English. To distinguish between aspirated and non-aspirated version of, say, p, try saying this pair of words:
- Pin (P is aspirated here)
- Spin (p is not aspirated here). The pronunciation mechanism of the unfamiliar [ʁ] is discussed under it.

2. Muteness

Most French consonants are never pronounced at the end of a word. There are only seven letters that are sometimes pronounced when they at the end of a word. They are c, f, l, r, p, s, k.

Factors Affecting Consonants

The behavior of consonants are modified by these processes.
1. Liaison: Consonants lose their muteness under certain conditions.
2. Gemination: Double consonants are pronounced as one elongated consonant under certain conditions.
3. Assimilation: Voiced consonants change to their voiced version and vice versa under certain conditions.

Chapter 14
[b] and [p]

[b]
This phoneme represents the sound of the letter b anywhere it is in a word except when followed by a voiceless consonant. In such a case, b has the sound /p/ instead.

Table 14.0: How [b] is Spelt in Words

Letters	Words
B, except when a voiced consonant follows immediately	Beurre Bain Hibou Robot Objet

[p]
This familiar plosive has acts as a liaison consonant with just two words: trop and beaucoup. Also, b has a [p] sound when a voiced consonant follows it immediately.
Par exemple : The b in the French absent actually has a [p] sound.

Table 14.1: How [p] is Spelt in Words

Letters	Words

P	Peine
• At the beginning of a word • Within a word • Between vowels	Pluie Peuple
B	Obtenir
• Followed by a voiced consonant	Absent Abstenir Absorber Abside

Chapter 15
[d] and [t]

[d]

This simple familiar consonant represents the letter d anywhere it is in a word except at the end of a word or liaison-eligible word boundaries.

Table 15.0: How [b] is Spelt in Words

Letters	Words
D • Everywhere except at the end of a word	Aide Diable Remède Demander Demain Décéder Découvrir Mesdames Dingue Fidèle Éducation Dangereuse Grande Froide Inde

[t]

This voiceless fricative is also a liaison consonant. When liaising a word that ends with a -d and another that starts with a vowel or a non aspirated H, the d changes to t.

Par exemple :

Grand ‿homme is pronounced /grɑ̃.tɔm/ and never /grɑ̃.dɔm/

Table 15.1: How [t] is Spelt in Words

Letters	Words
T or TT • At the beginning of • within a word (but **never** at the end)	Terre Tout Tour Jeter Cette Vite Partie Tête
Th	Thème Thé Théâtre Thaïlande Théorie Théorème Thyroïde Thèse Thym
T in -tion (provided -tion is preceded by s)	Gestion Question

Chapter 16
[ʃ] and [ʒ]

[ʃ]

This consonant phoneme, resembling the integral sign, serves to represent both ch- and sh-. It is the sound of the sh in "share". French lacks the affricate /tʃ/ used in English to distinguish chair from share.

Table 16.0: How [ʃ] is Spelt in Words

Letters	Words
Ch	Chanter
	Chemin
	Chaussures
	Chaise
Sh	Shampooing
	Shérif
	Short

[ʒ]

This phoneme is also called the soft g. It is the sound of g when followed by e or i. In verb conjugations, to maintain the softness of the g in the infinitive, an e is added before an end that

starts with a "hardener" like a to cancel out hardness.
Par exemple :
Je mangeais-----I was eating.
The real stem is mang- and the real ending is -ais. But 'mangais' would sound /mã.gɛ/ with a hard g instead of the soft g of the infinitive manger.
Hence, the intervention of the softening e.

Table 16.1: How It is Spelt in Words

Letters	Words
J	Jupe
	Jeune
	Jeter
	Jugement
	Jaune
	Jupe
	Jean
	Jardin
G + e or i	Manger
	Courge
	Gifle
	Dangereuse
	Changer
	Gêne
	Gène
	Genre
	Rouge
	Mariage

Chapter 17
[f] and [v]

[f]

This sound is the sound made by the letter f anywhere it is in a word. However, f has a /v/ sound at liaison-eligible word boundaries.

Table 17.0: How [f] is Spelt in Words

Letters	Words
f	Fleur
	Faille
	Fleuve
	Chef
	Neuf
	Café
	Chef
	Fumer
Ph	Physique
	Photo
	Phare
	Pharmacie
	Phase
	Phoque
	Philatélie
	Phénomène

[v]

This phoneme is a liaison consonant. When f occurs at a word boundary requiring liaison, it changes from /f/ to /v/

Par exemple :

Neuf‿ans is pronounced /nœ.vɑ̃/ and never /nœ.fɑ̃/

Table 17.1: How It is Spelt in Words

Letters	Words
V	Vin Voir Vous Voiture Épreuve Pouvoir Pleuvoir Avant
W	Wagon

Chapter 18
[g] and [k]

This sound is also called the hard g. It is the sound g has when followed by a, o, and u as in mango.

Table 18.0: How It is Spelt in Words

Letters	Words
G + a, o or u G in consonant clusters.	Gagner Gâteau Argot Grand Glauque
C (rare)	Second
Final g in some words	Iceberg

[k]

This familiar consonant also has the nickname of "hard c". It is the sound of c when followed by a, o or u and consonants. It is also the sound of c at the end of words. In verb conjugations, if stem of the infinitive has a terminal soft c, the soft is maintained in all conjugations. In this case, the softener is the cedilla accent.

Par exemple :

Nous commençons -----We begin.

The real stem is commenc- while the real ending is -ons. But to keep up the soft c of the infinitive commencer, a cedilla-accented c is used. Contrariwise, c remains hard at liaison-eligible word boundaries.
Par exemple:
Porc-épic is /pɔʁ.ke.pik/ and never /pɔʁ.se.pik/

Table 18.1: How [k] is Spelt in Words

Letters	Words
K	Kérosène
	Kilométrage
	Kiwi
	Koweït
C + a, o ,u and consonants	Carte
	Comme
	Vécu
C at the end of a word	Avec
	Sac
Q	Cinq
	Coq
Qu	Que
	Question
	Chaque
	Qui
	Manquer

Chapter 19
[l], [m] and [n]

[l]

This familiar sound gets pronounced when in certain positions in a word as shown below. /l/ is always clear, never pronounced like the last l in "little" ; rather, it is pronounced like the first.

Table 19.0: How [l] is Spelt in Words

Letters	Words
L at the end of a word	Jovial Journal Ciel Hôtel
L • Between vowels, • After consonants	Brûler Clé Joli
-ll-	Village Ville Distiller Elle

[m]

This is the familiar sound of the m in man.

This voiced nasal bilabial causes a vowel following it to become nasal provided there is no e in front of it.

Table 19.1: How [m] is Spelt in Words

Letters	Words
M • At the beginning of a word, • Between vowels	Même Mère Moi Mettre Métro
-mm-	Femme Homme

[n]

This is a nasal consonant which means air is made to pass through the nose in its production. It is also voiced. Apart from being a nasal itself, it nasalizes vowels that come behind provided there is no e in front.

Table 19.2: How It is Spelt in Words

Letters	Words
N • At the beginning of a word • Between vowels	Né Seine Peine Abdomen Amen

• At the end of some words	
-nn-	Benne Mécanicienne Bonne Mignonne Sienne Mienne Tienne
mn	Condamner Automne

Chapter 20
[ɲ] and [ŋ]

[ɲ]

This is the sound of the y in canyon. In other words, it is a nasalized [j]

*Table 20.0: How [ɲ] is Spelt in W*Word

Letters	Words
gn	Gagner Seigneur Signe Signature Signet Signifier. Ligne

[ŋ]

This is the sound of -ng in sing. This sound is not native to French. It is heard in words borrowed from English.

Table 20.1: How [ŋ] is Spelt in Words

Letters	Words
ng	Camping Shopping Jogging

Chapter 21
[ʁ]

This queer sound, an r sound made at the back of the throat, is not as hard as it appears. First off, it is made at the same place towards the back of the mouth as /g/ and /k/. Instead of the tightening and release of the uvular in /g/ or /k/, it is simply vibrated to make [ʁ].

Table 21.0: How [ʁ] is Spelt in Words

Letters	Words
R • Everywhere except at the end of -er verbs.	Rater Sur Croire Roi Pierre Finir Rouge

Chapter 22
[s] and [z]

[s]

This sound is the familiar sound of the s in see. It is also called the soft c. It is the sound of c when followed by e or i and also consider when c has the cedilla accent (ç)

Table 22.0: How [s] is Spelt in Words

Letters	Words
S • At the beginning of a word • Preceded by a consonant, provided the it is also followed by a consonant or mute e	Souffle Sortir Soir Sous Sur Seine Transe Transformer Savoir Suivre Sucre Triste Soudain
-ss-	Blesser Pressentir Intéresser Cassette

	Sagesse Casser
C + e or i (including all accented variants of e and i)	Cent Commencer Cédille Ancêtre Celte Céleste Décembre Décéder Ceci Cinéma
Ç	Commençons Tronçon Ça Reçu
T in -tion. (Provided -tion is not preceded by s)	Formation Éducation Solution Déclaration
X + consonant	Excéder Exprès Expérience Expatriée Excès
X at the end of a word.	Six Dix (These examples are exhaustive)
X within a word	Auxerre

| | Auxonne |
| | Bruxelles |

[z]

This voiced fricative serves as a liaison consonant for itself, s and x. At liaison-feasible word boundaries, s and x take on the [z] sound.

Par exemple :

Deux‿heures is pronounced /dø.zœ:ʁ/.

Table 22.1: How It is Spelt in Words

Letters	Words
Z • Everywhere except at the end of a word	Zéro
-s- between vowel sounds or vowel letters	Visiter Viser Thèse Transitif
X + vowel	Exercice Exaucé Examen Exemple

Phil Beth

SECTION IV

THE ROLE OF THE ACCENTS

Chapter 23
The Accents: Why They Matter .

Accents are signs placed on certain letters of the alphabet to show that the letter will sound differently from the usual, unaccented one. There are 5 accents used in French. They are shown in the table below.

Table 23.0: Accents Used in French

English	French	Symbols
The acute accent	L'accent aigu	é
The Grave Accent	L'accent grave	è, ù, à
The Cedilla	La cédille	ç
The Circumflex	Le circonflexe	â, ê, î, ô, û
The Dieresis	Le tréma	ï, ë

The Acute Accent
The acute accent, a forward-leaning stroke placed on the letter e, bestows the sound [e] upon an e. An acute-accented e is added to the stem of all -er

verbs including aller to make their past participles.
Examples:
Mangé
Phénomène
Écouté
Fermé
Né
Acheté
Côté
Donné
Café

The Grave Accent

This backward-leaning stroke is placed on a, e, and u. When placed on an e, it gives it the sound [ɛ] . When placed the other letters, pronunciation is not altered. With -er verbs,the grave accent is used in first person inversion of the imperfect tense of the subjunctive mood and present tense of the indicative mood as shown:
Je trouve. /ʒə.tʁu:v/ ------ I find (No inversion)
Trouvè-je? /tʁu:vɛ:ʒ/------Do I find? (Inversion)

Examples:
Père
Mère
Frère

Gère
Répète
Dernière
Achète
Lève

The Cedilla

This is the only accent placed on a consonant. The cedilla is the symbol that is under the c in ça. It confers an /s/ sound on a c that would otherwise sound /k/. When c is followed by a, o or u in French, it takes a /k/ sound and is said to be a hard c. In this book, the cedilla is referred to as a c softener because it turns a hard c (/k/) into a soft c (/s/).

Special Uses

Due to a need to preserve the softness of the c at end of some verb stems, the cedilla is used.

Examples

Nous form of commencer -- Nous commençons
The past participle of recevoir ---- Reçu.

Example Words:
Ça
Reçu
Tronçon
Leçon
Façon

Commençai

The Circumflex
The circumflex is the only accent that can be placed on all 5 vowel letters (â, ê, î, ô, û). With regard to pronunciation, the circumflex does not affect the pronunciation of i and u. It only serves to distinguish the spelling of the word from its unaccented double. E.g. du/dû, sur/sûr etc. However, it does change the sounds of a, e and o.

With a
The circumflex gives â an /ɑ/ ("back a") sound. Compare the following word pairs
Pâte /pɑt/ vs patte /pat/
Tâche /tɑʃ/ vs tache /taʃ/

With e
The circumflex gives ê an /ɛ/ sound. Compare the following word pairs:
Prêt /pʁɛ/ vs pré /pʁe/
Êtes /ɛt/ vs été /ete/

With o
The circumflex gives o the /o/ sound where it would otherwise be /ɔ/
Compare:
Côte /kot/ vs cote /kɔt/

The case of -eû-
It has been stated that the circumflex does not alter pronunciation with u. However, it does in the -eû- combination. Here, it changes the pronunciation from /œ/ to /ø/
Compare:
Jeune /ʒœn/ vs jeûne /ʒøn/

Words with the Circumflex:
Ancêtre
Hôpital
Hôtel
Frôler
Côte
Forêt
Tâche
Infâme
Âme
Être
Apôtre

The Dieresis
The dieresis serves to show that a vowel letter is not part of a digraph or diphthong. It shows that the vowel letter is in another syllable different from the vowel letter(s) adjacent to it.
Compare:
Air vs Haïr

***Examples**:*
Maïs
Noël
Citroën
Haïr
Taïga
Caraïbe
Canoë
Israël
Coïncider
Koweït
Naïf
Cap Haïtien
Haïti
Capharnaüm

SECTION V

SILENT LETTERS

Chapter 24
Silent Letters

French silent letters are letters (or cluster of letters) that are not pronounced except under certain conditions. They are usually found at the final position in words (except h which is silent at every position in a word).

The categories of silent letters are:
1. The unaccented e at the end of words with more than one syllable. It is also silent within some words. See list at under The Schwa.
2. All consonants are silent at the final position of words of any number of syllables (except c, b, f, k, q, l, s and r in some words). Note that l and r are only silent at the end of words if they are in -il and -er combinations respectively.
3. The -ent ending of third person plural forms of verbs.
4. U when preceded by g or q.

Situations in Which Silent Letters Lose their Muteness

1. All silent consonants lose their muteness during a liaison.
2. In French versification,(in poetry and music) the normally silent unaccented e comes back and takes on the schwa [ə] if the next word starts with a consonant.

Par exemple

Normally, n'existe pas is /nɛg.zist.pa/
But in a song, you would hear / nɛg.zis.tə.pa/

3. The final t in the -ent ending of third person plural forms of verbs is pronounced during an inversion.

Examples

Que veulent-ils ?
Parlent-ils l'anglais?
See the chapter on liaison for more explanation.

Chapter 25
Aspiration of H

The term aspirated H does not mean h produced as the aspirate /h/. French has two categories of words that start with h:
1. Words with h muet. (mute h)
2. Words with h aspirée (aspirated h)

In both cases, the h is silent.
So what is the aspirated h?
The aspirated h is an initial h found in words that are specifically marked as not allowing liaison and elision.

How to Identify the Aspirated H
Sadly, aspirated h words cannot be identified using any particular criteria. They simply have to be memorized. However, in some dictionaries, their phonetic transcriptions have a stress mark on the first syllable. A comprehensive list of aspirated h words are given at the end of this book.

Behavior of Aspirated H Words
Hiatus

Hiatus is a break in sound between vowels as a result of them occurring in adjacent syllables without an intervening consonant.

Since aspirated h words do not allow liaison, there is always a hiatus where a liaison consonant could have been. See the table below

Aspirated H Word	Pronunciation
Les Héros	[le.eʁo]
Des haricots	[de.aʁiko]
Les hiboux	[le.ibu]
Nous haïssons	[nu.aisɔ̃]
Vous haïssez	[vu.aise]

Zero Elision.

Aspirated h words never allow any form of contraction where an elision would normally occur. See examples in the table below:

Aspirated H	Pronunciation
Je hais	[ʒə.ɛ]
Le Havre	[lə.avʁ]
Le héro	[lə.eʁo]

SECTION VI

PRONUNCIATION ACROSS WORD BOUNDARIES AND THE ASSOCIATED PROCESSES

Chapter 26
Liaison

Simply put, liaison is the pronunciation of an otherwise silent word-final consonant because the following word begins with a vowel or an unaspirated h.

An English Example
Liaison is what we do with a final r in English: "For" is pronounced /fə/ , leaving r out but when it is followed by ever which has an initial vowel, we have /fərevə/. The dropped r is back again and the final r in ever is dropped. If we happen to have "for ever and ever", we say /fərevərən'evə/

However, French liaison is more than just picking up a dropped final consonant because the next word starts with a vowel. There are factors that determine liaison realization such as:
1. Linking or liaison consonants
2. Word associations or collocation.
3. Liaison restrictions.

Linking or Liaison Consonants
Linking or liaison consonants are the actual consonants that are inserted between two words in

which liaison occurs. For example, quand + on is supposed to be /kɑ̃.dɔ̃/ but it is not. This is because /d/ is never a liaison consonant. The correct pronunciation of quand on is /kɑ̃.tɔ̃/ They are as shown in the table below.

Table 26.0: Liaison Consonants

Liaison Consonant	Word Boundary	Examples
/j/	-il + vowel or mute h -ille + vowel or mute h	Gentil enfant. /ʒɑ̃.ti.j‿ɑ̃.fɑ̃/ Fille affable /fi.j‿afabl/
/k/	-c + vowel or mute h	Porc-épic /pɔʁ.k‿e.pik/
/g/	-g + vowel or mute h	Long article /lɔ̃.g‿aʁ.tikl/
/n/	-n + vowel or mute h	Un ami /œ̃.n‿a.mi/
/p/	-p + vowel or mute h	Trop élevé /tʁo.p‿el.ve/
/ʁ/	-r + vowel or mute h	Premier étage /pʁə.mjɛ.ʁ‿e.taʒ/
/t/	-d + vowel or mute h	Grand homme /gʁɑ̃.t‿ɔm/.

Phil Beth

	-t + vowel or mute h	Tout homme /tu.t‿ɔm/
/v/	-f + vowel or mute h	Neuf ans /nœ.v‿ã/
/z/	-s + vowel or mute h -z + vowel or mute h -x + vowel or mute h	Les enfants /le.z‿ã.fã/ Venez ici /və.ne.z‿i.si/ Faux amis /fo.z‿a.mi/

Word Associations or Collocation

A liaison is not made between just any two words of which one ends with a consonant and the other begins with a vowel. Liaison occurs mainly in word pairs that are frequently used. Examples of high frequency collocations include:

- Determiner + noun.
- Adjective+ noun
- Personal pronoun + verb.
- Fixed idiomatic compound words like États-Unis.

Liaison Restrictions

There are constraints regarding when to and when not to and when you could if you please, make a liaison. Hence there are :
1. Mandatory Liaison
2. Forbidden Liaison
3. Optional Liaison.

Phil Beth

Chapter 27
Mandatory Liaison

Mandatory liaisons are made compulsorily in certain word boundaries. The following are instances where liaison must be made:

1. ***Determiner + noun/ adjective that follows it.***

Examples :
Mon ami de Paris (My friend from Paris)
Un homme. (A man)
Ces arbres sont vieux. (These trees are old)
Les enfants
Deux oranges (Two oranges)
(For a comprehensive list of word categories classified as determiners, get my book "Do-It-Yourself French")

2. ***Subject/Object pronoun + verb and vice versa and also between two pronouns.***

Examples
Nous avons une maison
Vous êtes en retard.
Le temps vous endurcit de tout .
Le fin du monde nous a frôlé .
Quelle heure est-il ?
Est-elle contente ?
Nous y allons.
Nous en avons.

3. *In some fixed compound expressions like États-Unis, porc-épic, etc.*
4. *Adjective + noun*

Examples
Un bon ami.
Grand homme.
Un petit œuf.

5. *Adverb + the word it modifies*

Trop amusé
Assez intéressant.

6. *After a one-syllable preposition.*

Dans une maison.
En Inde
Chez elle

Chapter 28
Verb Conjugations and Liaison

Third Person Verb Inversion and Liaison

The third person subject pronouns (il, elle, on, ils, and elles) are frequently inverted with their verb forms. When this happens, the liaison consonant /t/ must be between the verb and the third-person pronoun. This is quite obvious as most third-person verb forms end in -d or -t.

Table 28.0: Third-person -Verb Inversion.

No Inversion	Inversion	Pronunciation
Il vend	Vend-il	/vã.til/
Elle vend	Vend-elle	/vã.tɛl/
On vend	Vend-on	/vã.tɔ̃/
Ils vendent	Vendent -ils	/vã.til/
Elles vendent	Vendent - elles	/vã.tɛl/
Il dort	Dort-il	/dɔʁ.til/
Elle dort	Dort-elle	/dɔʁ.tɛl/
On dort	Dort-on	/dɔʁ.tɔ̃/
Ils dorment	Dorment-ils	/dɔʁm.til/
Elles	Dorment-	/dɔʁm.tɛl/

| dorment | elles | |

From the table above, it makes sense that the liaison consonant is /t/ because when -d or -t occurs at a liaison-eligible word boundary, it must be /t/.

Now, there are third-person verb forms that end neither in t or d. When this is the case, in keeping with the third-person verb inversion rule, a -t- is mandatorily inserted between the verb and the third-person pronoun. See the table below:

Table 28.1: Third-person-Verb Inversion

No Inversion	Inversion
Il a	A-t-il
Elle a	A-t-elle
On a	A-t-on
Il va	Va-t-il
Elle va	Va-t-elle
On va	Va-t-on
Il s'appelle	S'appelle-t-il
Elle s'appelle	S'appelle-t-elle
On s'appelle	S'appelle-t-on
Il vainc	Vainc-t-il
Elle mange	Mange-t-elle
On danse	Danse-t-on
Il cherche	Cherche-t-il

First-Person-Singular -Verb Inversion and Liaison

Inversion with the first person singular pronoun is only found commonly in a few constructions as shown in the table below:

Table 28.2: Common 1st Person Singular Verb Inversions

Inversion	Pronunciation
Ai-je	/ɛːʒ/
Puis-je	/pɥiːʒ/
Suis-je	/sɥiːʒ/
Vais-je	/vɛːʒ/

Do you notice that the je is not pronounced /ʒə/ ? This is because in inversion, the subject and the verb are joined with a hyphen and pronounced as one word (and you know better than to pronounce the final unaccented e at the end of a word of more than one syllable)

First-Person-Singular -Verb Inversion in -er verbs

First person-verb inversion in -er verbs like parler, manger, etc are very rare. But if they ever occur, here is what happens: the final e of the first person singular form of the verb is changed to è as shown in the table below:

No inversion	Inversion	Pronunciation
Je parle	Parlè-je	/paʁlɛːʒ/
Je cache	Cachè-je	/kaʃɛːʒ/

The Imperative Mood and Liaison

Granted, basic knowledge of the imperative mood gives that er-ending verbs including aller lose their s in the second person singular.

Table 28.3: The Imperative

French	English
Mange!	Eat!
Danse!	Dance !
Saute!	Jump!
Chante !	Sing!

(For more explanation on the Imperative, get my book, "Do-It-Yourself French" where it is elaborately discussed)

But the liaison rule here says that if an imperative verb form is followed by the adverbial pronouns en or y, then the liaison consonant /z/ must be between the verb and en/y. This is obvious with imperative verb forms that end in -s or -z. In keeping with this rule, the lost -s in tu forms of the imperative pops back. See the table below:

Table 28.4: Imperative Inversion

Second-Person singular imperative without y/en	Second-Person singular imperative with y/en
Va !	Vas-y !
Donne !	Donnes-en !
Mange !	Manges-en !

Chapter 29
Forbidden and Optional Liaisons

Forbidden Liaison

There are certain cases in which liaison is downright unacceptable. (∅ between words shows liaison between them is forbidden)

1. *A subject that is not a subject pronoun + verb.*

Examples

Mes enfants ∅ ont envie de jouer au volley.
Les loups ∅ ont tué ses chiens.

2. *Direct object complement + indirect object complement*

J'ai donné les cadeaux ∅ à Pierre.
Je chante cette chanson ∅ và mon Dieu.

3. *Complete clause + Complete clause*

Example

Tu dors ∅ et je regarde.

4. *After et*

Example

Et ∅ en classe…
Elle a un chien et ∅ un chat.

5. *After a singular noun.*
Example
Son chat ∅ est mort hier.

6. *Before aspirated H words*
Des ∅ haricots
Les ∅ héros
Les ∅ hiboux

Liason Consonants After r: A Special Case
In some words, a liaison consonant is not pronounced after r.
Examples
Pars avec nous.
Fort agréable
Vers une solution.
However, this does not apply with plural nouns
Example
Nos jours heureux. (Our happy days)

Optional Liaison
Apart from the contexts listed under mandatory liaison and forbidden liaison, all others are

optional. However, choosing to make an optional liaison gives speech a tone of formality while choosing not to make it shows casualness. Common examples include

1. ***Auxiliary verb + past participle***

Example

Il est allé au cinéma hier soir.

2. ***Semi-auxiliary verb + infinitive.***

Je vais aller au stade.

3. ***After plural nouns***

Example

Mes blessures et mes faiblesses

4. ***Être in the present + adjective, adverb, or noun***

Example

Ils sont heureux.

5. ***After adverbs/prepositions with more than one syllable.***

Après avoir mangé.

Depuis un ans.

6. ***Verb + article/preposition/noun.***

Examples

 C'est un garçon.

Il vend une maison.

Chapter 30
Elision

Elision is the dropping of a vowel sound and replacing it with an apostrophe because of the fact that the next also starts with a vowel. This occurs mainly in one-syllable words. In French, elision occurs with the final e of monosyllabic words. An exception is the elision of the I in si when the next word is il or ils.

Mandatory Elisions

Elision is compulsory in the following constructions:

1. ***The definite articles le / la + vowel/ mute h*** e.g.

le + arbre → l'arbre
la + église → l'église

2. ***The subject pronouns je and ce + vowel/mute h***

J'habite à Dakar.
C'est génial.

3. ***The object pronouns me, te, se, le, and la***

Jean s'est rasé, l'a vue, m'a téléphoné. ("Jean shaved himself, saw her, phoned me.")

4. The object pronouns le, la, moi, toi when they occur after an imperative verb and before the pronoun en or y:

Mettez-l'y, donne-m'en, va-t'en. ("Put it there, give me some, leave.")

5. Negative marker ne + vowel

Elle n'arrête pas de parler. ("She won't stop talking.")

6. The preposition de + vowel

Le père d'Albert vient d'arriver.

7. Que + vowel

Qu'as-tu dit ? Qu'il ne nous restait plus qu'une semaine.

8. The conjunction si + the pronouns il and ils

S'il vous plaît.
S'ils gagnent, ils recevront des prix.

Phil Beth

Chapter 31
Enchaînement

Enchaînement comes from the verb enchaîner which means to chain. So enchaînement means linking successive words in a rhythmic pattern to avoid inelegant pauses between words. Using enchaînement in speech is a sign of fluency or mastery. It takes one's French from sounding like a toddler's holophrastic babbling to a masterful, well-produced speech.

Mechanism of Enchaînement
Enchaînement occurs within rhythmic groups. Words within a rhythmic group are chained together as though they were one word.
Since French prefers open syllables to closed ones, to avoid having closed syllables all over the place, the final pronounced consonant of a word is transferred to the vowel-initial word that follows within a rhythmic group.

Types of Enchaînement.
1. Consonantal Enchaînement
2. Vocalic Enchaînement

Consonantal Enchaînement

Phil Beth

This happens when a pronounced final consonant is transferred to the next word which begins with a vowel.

Table 31.0: Consonantal Enchaînement

Rhythmic Group	Pronunciation
Avec elle	A-ve-kel
Elle est	El- leh

Vocalic Enchaînement

This happens when a vowel ends a word and a vowel begins the next word also. Instead of pausing between the two words, they are said as if they were in one word.

Table 31.1: Vocalic Enchaînement

Rhythmic Group	Pronunciation
Il a eu	[i.lay]
J'ai acheté	[ʒɛaʃte]

Chapter 32
Gemination

Gemination means lengthening a consonant. In English, it occurs in words like bookkeeping where we have a double k. To effect gemination, we hold our breath at the first k, pause a bit and then release it at the second k.

In French, gemination is particularly important for elimination of confusion in identical constructions.

Par exemple

Il l'a mangé vs il a mangé.

It is tempting to read both the same way but that would be quite confusing.

In Il l'a mangé, the /ll/ has to be lengthened to contrast it from the /l/ in il a mangé.

Gemination is also necessary to differentiate the conditional forms of mourir and courir from the imperfect forms.

Table 32.0: Mourir and Courir in the Conditional and Imperfect

	Conditional	Imperfect
Mourir	Je mourrais	Je mourais
	Tu mourrais	Tu mourais
	Il/Elle mourrait	Il/Elle mourait
	Nous	Nous

	mourrions	mourions
	Vous mourriez	Vous mouriez
	Ils/Elle mourraient	Ils/Elle mouraient
Courir	Je courrais	Je courais
	Tu courrais	Tu courais
	Il/Elle courrait	Il/Elle courait
	Nous courrions	Nous courions
	Vous courriez	Vous couriez
	Ils/Elles courraient	Ils/Elles couraient

SECTION VII

INTONATION AND STRESS

Chapter 33
Intonation and Stress

Intonation is the pitch of the voice in speech. The pitch of the voice varies depending on the type of statement we are making, whether it is a factual statement, an educated-guess question, a WH-question or an exclamation. There are 3 types of intonation patterns in French pronunciation:

The Rising Intonation
In this pattern, the pitch of the voice rises progressively throughout the sentence and never falls.
This intonation pattern is found in Yes /No questions.
Example.
1. N'est-ce pas?
2. Ai-je tort?
3. N'y a-t-il pas d'eau?
4. Vous voulez du riz?
5. Tu es français ?
6. A-t-il des frères et sœurs ?
7. Tu vas avec moi ou non?
8. Tu as besoin de l'argent?
9. Nous allons au Nigéria demain ?
10. C'est une prière ?

Phil Beth

The Falling Intonation
In falling intonation, the pitch of the voice falls progressively throughout the sentence and never rises. It is heard in short declarative sentences, orders and exclamations.
Examples
1. Je mange du riz.
2. Il est français..
3. C'est un garçon.
4. Allons-y !
5. On y va
6. Viens ici !
7. Quelle surprise !
8. J'arrive!
9. À la prochaine !
10. Que Dieu te bénisse !

Rise-fall Intonation
In this pattern, the pitch of the voice rises at the beginning of the sentence and falls towards the end. It is heard in long declarative sentences and WH- questions. (WH- questions are questions that begin with the question markers: How, What, When, Why, Which, etc. They are also called information questions.) To learn more about WH- questions in French, get my book "Do-It-Yourself French"

1. Les nouvelles disent que la reine est morte la nuit dernière.
2. Si j'avais su, je ne l'aurais pas acheté.
3. Si on gagne, on recevra des prix.
4. Que veux-tu ?
5. Quand arrivez-vous ?
6. Où est-ce ?
7. Pourquoi les gens se battent ?
8. Qu'est-ce que c'est?
9. Quelle heure est-il ?
10. Combien de fois la fin du monde nous a frôlé.

Stress

Stress is not as significant in French as it is in English. Stress is placed on the final full syllable of a word. A full syllable is one whose vowel is not the schwa.

SECTION VIII

EXCEPTIONS TO COMMON RULES

Chapter 34
Irregular Pronunciation Patterns

Generally speaking, pronunciation is irregular—there is no definitive rule for it. This because French pronunciation is not orthographic, that is to say, words are not said the way they are spelt. Irregularities in French pronunciation are due to a multiplicity of factors including

- Etymology: French is a Romance language which means it is from Latin. As words undergo modifications from their Latin 'ancestors', complex orthographic and phonological changes occur.
- Loan words: Words that are borrowed from other languages and therefore keep their original pronunciation. (Examples: jean, week-end, western etc)
- Brand names: Trademarks from other languages e.g. Jeep, Walkman, etc.

There are some words that do not follow the general pronunciation patterns. That is to say, their pronunciation cannot be accurately inferred from their spelling using common patterns.

Table 34.0: Irregular Pronunciation

Words	Pronunciation
Sept	[sɛt]
Fils	[fis]
Porc	[pɔʁ]
Gentil	[ʒɑ̃ti]
Coffre	[kɔʁ]
Coïncider	[kɔɛ̃side]
Oasis	[ɔazis]
Summum	[sɔmɔm]
Ours	[uʁs]
Sélect	[selɛct]
Montréal	[mɔ̃ʁeal]
Parasol	[paʁasol]
Syphilis	[sifilis]
Wagon	[vagɔ̃]
Est	[ɛst]
Koweït	[kɔwejt]
Album	[albɔm]
Baptême	[batɛm]
Cap	[kap]

Chapter 35
Informal Pronunciation

Informal French is different from Standard French in many ways including pronunciation. We will discuss them under the following:
1. Elision
2. Assimilation
3. Liaison

Elision
Elisions are made where they would never be made in careful speech.

Table 35.0: Informal Elision

Standard Usage	Informal Usage
Tu as	T'as
Tu es	T'es
Je n'ai pas	J'n'ai pas
Ce que	C'que

Assimilation
In some cases, informal elision leads to a voiced consonant following an unvoiced one which in turn necessitates assimilation.

Table 35.1: Informal Assimilation

Elision	Assimilation

Je suis = J'suis	Chuis.
Je sais = J'sais	Chais.

Liaison

In informal French, all optional liaisons are not made so as not to sound too serious.

Phil Beth

Chapter 36
Cases of Special Pronunciation

Inversion
In a subject pronoun-verb inversion, the resulting hyphenated compound word is pronounced like one word and follows the rules of pronunciation for words.
Example
Ai-je is pronounced as it would be if it were one word aije, that is, the last e is not pronounced.

Third Person Plural Verb Conjugations
The -ent ending of third person plural forms is just like a mute e —it is never pronounced.
Example
Peuvent is pronounced as if it were 'peuve'
Parlent is exactly pronounced like parle.

Phil Beth

APPENDIX
Full List of Aspirated H Words
(Source: Wikipedia)

Words beginning with ha

- habanera (n. f.)
- hâbler (v. tr. ou intr.)
- hâblerie (n. f.)
- hâbleur, -euse (adj. ou n. m./f.)
- hache (n. f.)
- hache-écorce (n. m. sing.)
- hache-écorces (n. m. pl.)
- hache-fourrage (n. m. invar.)
- hache-légume
- hall (n. m.)
- halle (n. f.)
- hallebarde (n. f.)
- hallebardier (n. m.)
- hallier (n. m.)
- hallstatien, -ienne (adj. m./f.)
- halo (n. m.)
- haloir or hâloir (n. m.)
- halophile (adj. or n. m.)
- halot (n. m.)
- halte (n
- harceler (v. tr.)
- harcèlement (n. m.)
- harceleur, -euse (n. or adj. m./f.)
- hachichich (n. m.)
- harde (n. f.)
- harder (v.
- haubanan (n. m.)
- haubanner (v. tr.)
- haubanneur, -euse (n. or adj. m./f.)
- hauberge on (n. m.)
- ha

A Handbook of Oral French

- s (n. m. invar.)
- hache-maïs (n. m. invar.)
- hache-paille (n. m. invar.)
- hacher (v. tr.)
- hachereau, -eaux (n. m. sing./pl.)
- hache-sarment (n. m. sing. or pl.)
- hache-sarments (n. m. pl.)
- hachette (n. f.)
- hache-viande (n. m. invar.)
- hachage (n. m.)
- . f.)
- hamac (n. m.)
- hamada (n. f.)
- hamal or hammal (n. m.)
- Hambourg (n. propre m.)
- hamburger (n. m.)
- hameau, -eaux (n. m. sing./pl.)
- hammal or hamal (n. m.)
- hammam (n. m.)
- hammerless (n. m.)
- hampe (n. f.)
- hamster (n. tr.)
- hardes (n. f. pl.)
- hardi (adj.)
- hardiesse (n. f.)
- hardiment (adv.)
- hardware (n. m. anglicisme)
- harem (n. m.)
- hareng (n.
- ubert (n. m.)
- hausse (n. f.)
- hausse-col (n. m.)
- haussement (n. m.)
- hausse-pied (n. m.)
- hausser (v. tr.)
- hausseur

- *hacheur, -euse* (adj. or n. m./f.)
- *hachis* (n. m.)
- *hachich* (n. m.)
- *hachisch* (n. m.)
- *hachoir* (n. m.)
- *hachure* (n. f.)
- *hack* (n. m. anglicisme)
- *hacquebute* ou *haquebute* (n. f.)
- *hacquebutier* ou *haquebutier* (n. m.)
- *hadal, -aux* (adj. sing./pl.)
- *haddock* (n. m.)
- *han!* (interj. or n. m.)
- *hanap* (n. m.)
- *hanche* (n. f.)
- *hanchement* (n. m.)
- *hancher* (v. tr. or intr. or pr.)
- *hand* (n. m., abrév.)
- *handball* or *hand-ball* (n. m.)
- *handballeur, -euse* (n. m./f.)
- *handicap* (n. m.)
- *handicaper* (v. tr.)
- *hangar* (n. m.)
- *hareng* (n. m.)
- *harengère* (n. f.)
- *haret* (adj. m.)
- *harfang* (n. m.)
- *hargne* (n. f.)
- *hargneux, -euse* (adj. m./f.)
- *hargneusement* (adv.)
- *haricot* (n. m.)
- *harengeuse* (n. or adj. m./f.)
- *haussement* (adv.)
- *haussier* (n. m.)
- *haussier, -ière* (adj. m./f.)
- *haut* (adj.)
- *hauta*

A Handbook of Oral French

- *k* (n. m.)
- *hadîth* (n. m.)
- *hadj* (n. m.)
- *hadji* (n. m.)
- *haguais* (adj.)
- *Haguais, -aise* (n. m./f.)
- *Hague, la* (n. propre f.)
- *hagard* (adj.)
- *ha ! ha !* (interj.)
- *haha* (n. m.)
- *hahé !* (interj. or n. m.)
- *haie* (n. f.)
- *haïe* (part. pass. de *haïr*)
- *hanneton* (n. m.)
- *hannetonner* (v. tr. or intr.)
- *hanse* (n. f.)
- *hanséatique* (adj.)
- *hanter* (v. tr.)
- *hantise* (n. f.)
- *happe* (n. f.)
- *happelourde* (n. f.)
- *happer* (v. tr.)
- *happening* (n. m. anglicisme)
- *happement* (n. m.)
- *happy-end* or *happy end* (n. m.)
- *haricoter* (v. tr.)
- *haridelle* (n. f.)
- *harissa* (n. f.)
- *harka* (n. f.)
- *harki* (n. m.)
- *harle* (n. m.)
- *harlou !* (interj. n. m.)
- *harnacher* (v. tr.)
- *in* (n. m.)
- *hautain, -aine* (adj.)
- *hautbois* (n. m.)
- *haut-de-chausses* (n. m. sing.)
- *haut-de-forme* (n. m. sing.)
- *ha*

Phil Beth

- *haïk* (n. m.)
- *haillon* (n. m.)
- *haillonneux, -euse* (adj. or n. m./f.)
- *haine* (n. f.)
- *haineux, -euse* (adj. m./f.)
- *haineusement* (adv.)
- *haïr* (v. tr.)
- *haïssable* (adj.)
- *halage* (n. m.)
- *halbran* (n. m.)
- *hâle* (n. m.)
- *halecret* (n. m.)
- *haler* (v. tr.)
- *hâler* (v. intr.)
- *haleter*
- anglicisme)
- *haquebute* or *hacquebute* (n. f.)
- *haquebutier* or *hacquebutier* (n. m.)
- *haquenée* (n. f.)
- *haquet* (n. m.)
- *hara-kiri* (n. m.)
- *harangue* (n. f.)
- *haranguer* (v. tr.)
- *harangueur, -euse* (n. m./f.)
- *haras* (n. m.)
- *harassant* (adj.)
- *harasse*
- *harnacheur, -euse* (n. or adj. m./f.)
- *harnachement* (n. m.)
- *harnais* (n. m.)
- *harnois* (n. m. vieux)
- *haro !* (interj. or n. m.)
- *harpail*
- *ute-contre* (n. m./f. sing.)
- *haute-forme* (n. m. sing.)
- *hautement* (adv.)
- *hautesse* (n. f.)
- *hauteur* (n. f.)
- *haute*

- *halètement* (n. m.)
- *harasser* (v. tr.)
- *harassement* (n. m.)
- *harpe* (n. f.)
- *harper* (v. tr. or intrans.)
- *harpie* (n. f.)
- *harpiste* (n. m. or f.)
- *harpon* (n. m.)
- *harponner* (v. ler, se (v. pronom.)
- *hauts-contre* (n. m./f. pl.)
- *hautes-formes* (n. m. pl.)
- *haut-fond* (n. m. sing.)
- *hautin* (n. m.)
- *haut-le-cœur* (n. m. inv

- *harponneur, -euse* (n. or adj. m./f.)
- *harponnage* (n. m.)
- *hart* (n. f. vieux)
- *hasard* (n. m.)
- *hasarder* (v. tr. or pr.)
- *hasardeux,*
- *haut-le-corps* (n. m. inv ar.)
- *haut-le-pied* (n. m. or adj. or adv. inv ar.)
- *haut-parleur* (n. m. sing.)
- *haut-par*

- -euse (adj. m./f.)
- hasardeusement (adv.)
- haschich (n. m.)
- hase (n. f.)
- hast (n. m. vieil.)
- hastaire (n. m.)
- haste (n. f.)
- hât leurs (n. m. pl.)
- haut-relief (n. m. sing.)
- hauts-de-chaussees (n. m. pl.)
- hauts-de-forme (n. m. pl.)
- hauts-fon

- *hâtelet* (n. f.)
- *hâtelet* (n. m.)
- *hâtelette* (n. f.)
- *hâter* (v. tr. or pr.)
- *hâtier* (n. m.)
- *hâtif, -ive* (adj. m./f.)
- *hâtiveau* (n. m.)
- *hâtivement*
- *hauts-fonds* (n. m. pl.)
- *hauts-reliefs* (n. m. pl.)
- *hauturier, -ière* (adj. m./f.)
- *havage* (n. m.)
- *havanais* (adj.)
- *Havanais, -aise* (

(adv.)
- *havane* (n.m.)
- *Havane, la* (n. propre f.)
- *hâve* (n.m.)
- *haveneau* (n.m.)
- *havenet* (n.m.)
- *haver* (v.tr.)
- *haveur, -*

n. m./f.)

- *haveuse* (n. m./f.)
- *havir* (v. tr. or pro nom.)
- *havrais* (adj.)
- *Havrais, -aise* (n. m./f.)
- *havre* (n. m.)
- *Havre, le* (n. pro pre m.)

- *havresac* or *havre-sac* (n. m. sing.)
- *havresacs* or *havre-sacs* (n. m. pl.)
- *hayon* (n. m.)

Words beginning with *he*

- *hé !* (interj. or n. m.)
- *heaume* (n. m.)
- *heau
- *hennir* (v. intr.)
- *hennissant* (adj.)
- *hennissement* (n. m.)
- *hérisser* (v. tr.)
- *hérisseur, -euse* (adj. or n. m./f.)
- *hérisso
- *herse* (n. f.)
- *herser* (v. tr.)
- *hertz* (

- mier (n. m.)
- hé bien! (interj. or n. m.)
- heimatlos (adj. et n. invar.)
- hein ? (interj. or n. m.)
- hélas ! (interj. or loc. adv.)[1]
- héler (v. tr.)
- héleur, -euse (n. or adj. m./f.)
- hennisseur, -euse (n. or adj. m./f.)
- Henri, -iette (n. propre m./f.)
- henry (n. m.)
- Henry (n. propre m.)
- hep ! (interj. or n. m.)
- héraut (n. m.)
- herchage or herschage (n. m.)
- hercher or herscher (v. tr.)
- hercheur, -euse or n (n. m.)
- hérissonner (v. tr.)
- hermitique (adj.)
- herniaire (adj. or n. f.)
- hernie (n. f.)
- hernieux, -euse (adj. m./f.)
- héron (n. m.)
- héronnier, -ière (adj. m./f.)
- héros (n. m.)
- herschage or herchage (n. m.)
- herscher or hercher (v. tr.)
- n. m. invar.)
- hertzien, -ienne (adj. m./f.)
- hêtraie (n. f.)
- hêtre (n. m.)
- heu .../heux (interj. or n. m. sing./pl.)
- heulandite

- hèlement (n. m.)
- hello : (interj. or n. m.)
- hem ! or hum ! (interj. or n. m.)
- hemloc or hemlock (n. m.)
- henné (n. m.)
- herscheur, -euse (n. m./f.)
- hère (n. m.)
- hérissement (n. m.)
- herscheur, -euse or hercheur, -euse (n. m./f.)
- (n. f.)
- heurt (n. m.)
- heurtement (n. m.)
- heurtequin (n. m.)
- heurter (v. tr. or pr.)
- heurteur, -euse (n. or adj. m./f.)
- heu

rtoir (n. m.)

Words beginning with *hi*

- *hi !* (interj. ou n. m.)
- *hiatal, -aux* (adj. sing./pl.)
- *hiatus* (n. m. invar.)
- *hibou, -oux* (n. m. sing./pl.)
- *hic !* (interj. ou n. m.)
- *hic et nunc* (loc. adv.)
- *hickory, -ies* (n. m.
- *hiératique* (adj.)
- *hiératiquement* (adv.)
- *hiératisant* (adj.)
- *hiératisé* (adj.)
- *hiératisme* (n. m.)
- *hiérochromie* (n. f.)
- *hiérocrate* (n. m.)
- *hiérocratisme* (n. m.)
- *hiérodrame* (n. m.)
- *hiérogamie* (n. f.)
- *hiéroga*
- *hiérogramme* (n. m.)
- *hiérogrammate* (n. m.)
- *hiérogrammatisme* (n. m.)
- *hiérographe* (n. m.)
- *hiéromancie* (n. f.)
- *hiéromoine* (n. m.)
- *hiérophanie* (n. f.)
- *hiloire* (n. f.)
- *Hilbert* (n. propre m.)
- *Hildegarde* (n. propre f.)
- *hindi* ou *hindî* (adj. ou n. m.)
- *hip hip hip !* (interj.)

A Handbook of Oral French

- sing./pl.)
- hidalgo (n. m.)
- hideur (n. f.)
- hideusement (adv.)
- hideux, -euse (adj. m./f.)
- hie (n. f.)
- hiement (n. m.)
- hier (v. intr.)
- hiérocéphale (adj.)
- hiérarchie (n. f.)
- hiérarchique (adj.)
- hiérarchiquement (adv.)
- hiérarmique (adj.)
- hiéroglyphe (n. m.)
- hiéroglyphé (adj.)
- hiéroglyphie (n. f.)
- hiéroglyphié (adj.)
- hiéroglyphique (adj.)
- hiéroglyphiquement (adv.)
- hiéroglyphisme (n. m.)
- hiéroglyphite (n. m.)
- hiéroscopie (n. f.)
- hiéroscopique (adj.)
- hi-fi (loc. adj. abbrév. invar.)
- highlandais, -aise (adj. m./f.)
- Highlander (n. m.)
- Highlands (n. propre m. pl.)
- high-life (n. m. anglicisme)
- hip-hop (n. m. ou adj. invar.)
- hippie ou hippy, -ies (n. m. ou f. ou adj. sing./pl. anglicisme)
- hissage (n. m.)
- hisser (v. tr. ou pr.)
- hissement (

- *chiser* (v. tr.)
- *hiérarchisation* (n. f.)
- *highlifer* (v. intr. anglicisme)
- *highlifeur* (n. m. anglicisme)
- *hi-han !* ou *hi han !* (interj. ou n. m.)
- *hilaire* (adj.)
- *Hilaire* (n. propre m.)
- *hile* (n. m.)
- n. m.)
- *hisseur, -euse* (n. ou adj. m./f.)
- *histoire* (n. f.)
- *hit* (n. m., anglicisme)
- *hit-parade* (n. m. sing., anglicisme)
- *hit-parades* (n. m.

A Handbook of Oral French

- hittite (adj. ou n. m.)
- Hittite (n. m./f.)

Words beginning with *ho*

- *ho !* (interj. ou n. m.)
- *Hobart* (n. propre m.)
- *hobby, -ies* (n. m. sing./pl.)
- *hobereau, -eaux* (n. m.
- *Hollywood* (n. propre m.)
- *hollywoodesque* (adj.)
- *hollywoodien, -ienne* (adj.)
- *hom
- *hors-bord* (loc. adj. ou n. m. sing.)
- *hors-bords* (n. m. pl.)
- *hors-caste* (n. m. sing.)
- *houle* (n. f.)
- *houler* (v. intr.)
- *houlette* (n. f.)
- *houleux, -euse* (adj. m./f.)
- *houleusement* (adv.)
- *houlier* (n. m.)

- sing./pl.)
- *hobereautaille* (n. f.)
- *hoberelle* (n. f.)
- *hoc* (n. m.)
- *hoca* (n. m.)
- *hocco* ou *hocko* (n. m.)
- *hoche* (n. f.)
- *hochement* (n. m.)
- *hochepot* (n. m.)
- *hochequeue* ou *hoche-queue* (n.
- *ard* (n. m.)
- *homarderie* (n. f.)
- *homardier* (n. m.)
- *home* (n. m. anglicisme)
- *homespun* (n. m. angl.)
- *hon !* (interj. ou n. m.)
- *Honduras, le* (n. propre m.)
- *hondurien*
- *hors-castes* (n. m. pl.)
- *hors-d'œuvre* ou *hors d'œuvre* (n. m. invar.)
- *horse guard* ou *horse-guard* (n. m. sing.)
- *horse guards* ou *horse-guards* (n. m. pl.)
- *horse-*
- *houlque* ou *ouque* (n. f.)
- *houp !* (interj. ou n. m.)
- *houppe* (n. f.)
- *houppelande* (n. f.)
- *houppette* (n. f.)
- *houppier* (n. m.)
- *houque* ou *oulque* (n. f.)
- *hourailis* (n. m. invar.)
- *hourd* (n. m.)
- *hourdage* (n. m.)
- *hourder* (v. tr.)
- *hourdi*

A Handbook of Oral French

- m. sing.)
- *hochequeues* ou *hoche-queues* (n. m. pl.)
- *hocher* (v. tr.)
- *hochet* (n. m.)
- *hockey* (n. m.)
- *hockeyeur, -euse* (n. m./f.)
- *hocko* ou *hocco* (n. m.)
- *hodja* (n. m.)
- *hoffmannes (adj.)
- *Hondurien, -ienne* (n. m./f.)
- *hongre* (n. m.)
- *hongreline* (n. f.)
- *hongrer* (v. tr.)
- *hongreur, -euse* (n. m./f.)
- *Hongrie, la* (n. propre f.)
- *hongrois* (adj. ou n. pox (n. m. invar.)
- *hors-jeu* (n. m. invar.)
- *hors-la-loi* (n. invar.)
- *hors-série* (n. m. ou adj. invar.)
- *horst* (n. m. invar.)
- *hors-texte* (n. m. invar.)
- *hosanna, -is* (n. m. sing./pl.)
- *hourdis* (n. m. invar.)
- *houret* (n. m.)
- *houri* (n. f.)
- *hourque* (n. f.)
- *hourra !* ou *hurra !* (interj. ou n. m.)
- *hourvari* (n. m.)
- *houseau, -eaux* (n. m. sing./pl.)
- *houspiller* (v. tr.)
- *houspilleur, -*

Phil Beth

- *que* (adj.)
- *hoffmannien, -ienne* (adj. m./f.)
- *hognement* (n. m.)
- *hogner* (v. intr.)
- *holà !* (interj. ou n. m. ou n. f. invar.)
- *holding* (n. f.)
- *hôler* (v. intr.)
- *hold-up* (n. m.)
- *hollandais* (adj.)
- *Hollaque* (adj.)
- *Hongrois, -se* (n. m./f.)
- *hongroyage* (n. m.)
- *hongroyer* (v. tr.)
- *hongroyeur, -euse* (n. m./f.)
- *honnir* (v. tr.)
- *honnissement* (n. m.)
- *honte* (n. f.)
- *honteux, -euse*
- *Hong* (n. m.)
- *as* ou *hosannah, -hs* (n. m.)
- *hosannière* (adj. f.)
- *hotdog* ou *hot-dog* (n. m. sing.)
- *hotdogs* ou *hot-dogs* (n. m. pl.)
- *hotte* (n. f.)
- *hottée* (n. f.)
- *hotter* (v. tr.)
- *euse* (adj. ou n. m./f.)
- *houspillement* (n. m.)
- *houssage* (n. m.)
- *houssaie* (n. f.)
- *housse* (n. f.)
- *housser* (v. tr.)
- *houssine* (n. f.)
- *houssoir* (n. m.)
- *Houston* (n. propre f.)
- *houx* (n. m. invar.)
- *hoyau, -aux* (n. m.

- *hollandais, -aise* (n. m./f.)
- *hollandaisement* (adv.)
- *hollande* (n. m. ou f.)
- *Hollande, la* (n. propre f.)
- *hollandé* (adj.)
- *hollandiser* (v. tr.)
- *hollando-belge* (adj.)
- *hollando-français, -aise* (adj. m./f.)
- *hontuesement* (adv.)
- *hop !* (interj.)
- *hoquet* (n. m.)
- *hoqueter* (v. intr. ou tr.)
- *hoquètement* (n. m.)
- *hoqueton* (n. m.)
- *horde* (n. f.)
- *horion* (n. m.)
- *hor- hottentot, -ote* (adj. ou n. m./f.)
- *hotteur, -euse* (n. m./f.)
- *hou !* (interj. ou n. m.)
- *houp !* (interj. ou n. m.)
- *houblon* (n. m.)
- *houblonner* (v. tr.)
- *houblonneur, -euse* sing./pl.)

- hollando-norvégien, -ienne (adj. m./f.)
- hollando-saxon, -onne (adj. m./f.)
- mis (prép.)
- hornblende (n. f.)
- hors (prép. ou adv.)
- horsain (n. m.)
- (n. m./f.)
- houblonnière (n. f.)
- houdan (n. f.)
- Houdan (n. propre m.)
- houe (n. f.)
- houhou (n. m.)
- houille (n. f.)
- houiller, -ère (adj. m./f.)
- houillère (n. f.)
- houilleux, -

- *euse* (adj. m./f.)
- *houka* (n. m.)

Words beginning with *hu*

- *huard* (n. m.)
- *hublot* (n. m.)
- *huche* (n. f.)
- *huchée* (n. f.)
- *hucher* (v. tr. ou pr.)
- *huchet* (n. m.)
- *huchier* (n. m.)
- *hue !* (interj. ou n. m.)
- *huée* (n. f.)
- *huer* (v. tr. ou pr.)
- *huerta, -*
- *hugotique* (adj.)
- *hugotisme* (n. m.)
- *Hugues, -ette* (n. propre m./f.)
- *huguenot, -ote* (n. ou adj. m./f.)
- *huis-clos* ou *huis clos* (n. m. invar.)
- *huit* (adj. ou n. invar.)
- *huitai*
- *humer* (v. tr.)
- *humeux, -euse* (adj. m./f.)
- *humoter* (v. tr.)
- *hune* (n. f.)
- *hunier* (n. m.)
- *hunter* (n. m. anglicisme)
- *huppe* (n. f.)
- *huppé* (ad
- *Huro-iroquois, -oise* (n. m./f.)
- *huron, -onne* (adj. m./f.)
- *Huron, -onne* (n. m./f.)
- *Huronien* (n. m.)
- *huronien, -ienne* (adj.

A Handbook of Oral French

- *as* (n. f.)
- *huehau !* (interj. ou n. m.)
- *Hugo* (n. propre m.)
- *hugolâtre* (adj.)
- *hugolâtrie* (n. f.)
- *hugolien, -ienne* (adj. m./f.)

- *n* (n. m.)
- *huitaine* (n. f.)
- *huitante* (n. f.)
- *huitième* (adj. ou n. m. ou f.)
- *Hulk, -ette* (n. propre m./f.)
- *hulotte* (n. f.)
- *hululation* (v. tr.)
- *hululer* (v. tr.)
- *hum !* (interj. ou n.m.)
- *humage* (n. m.)
- *humement* (n. m.)

- j.)
- *huque* (n. f.)
- *hure* (n. f.)
- *hurlade* (n. f.)
- *hurlée* (n. f.)
- *hurlement* (n. m.)
- *hurler* (v. tr.)
- *hurleur, -euse* (adj. m./f.)
- *huro-iroquois, -oise* (adj. m./f.)

- m./f.)
- *hurricane* (n. m.)
- *husky, -ies'* (n. m.)
- *hussard* (n. m. ou adj.)
- *hussite* (n. m.)
- *hussitisme* (n. m.)
- *hutin* (n. ou adj. m.)
- *hutinet* (n. m.)
- *hutte* (n. f.)
- *hutteau* (n. m.)

Phil Beth

- *hutter* (v. tr.)
- *huttier* (n. m.)